FALLING FORWARD: A LYRICAL MEMOIR

FALLING FORWARD: A LYRICAL MEMOIR

Braulio Fonseca

Falling Forward: A Lyrical Memoir

ISBN: 979-8-89933-021-6 (Paperback)
Library of Congress Control Number: 2026904936

Cover Design: Erin Mann
Book Design: Virgil Suarez

Printed in the United States of America.
First printing 2026.

Redhawk Publications
The Catawba Valley Community College Press
2550 Hwy 70 SE
Hickory, NC 28602
https://redhawkpublications.com

This memoir is dedicated to Nancy Schuele
and Silvia Marta Herrera Sanchez de Fonseca

A writer who has power should
use it to extract such benefits from his
publisher as give his words room to breathe.
I want my words to strike like a snake
A snake can't strike in a box.

—Norman Mailer

TABLE OF CONTENTS

PART I

FAILING

2020/2021

The rain always seems to clean Los Angeles.

It
always seems to

D

R

I

P

D

O

W
N

on to the streets
as if it were erasing the
filth
and eradicating the brown hazy viscousness of the air,

but only for the moment it falls.

It's been raining for days now, weeks maybe,
it's hard to remember.

One thing is for certain -

The corner of Figueroa and 41st has never smelled so fresh

and looked so clean.

Let it rain.

Let it rain. Let it rain.

Let it rain. Let it rain. Let it rain.

The world is dying – or so they say

but I look around these LA streets and
the death that
is always present
seems more alive now – more than ever.

Invisible zombies that hide in the light
have found refuge
in the exiled city
and they now run amuck. Wild.

I join them
as I take one final walk downtown,
one final stretch of my legs,
one final look at this city that has been my home.

I pass Martin Luther King Jr. Blvd and see Tom's Jr. – Closed.

I pass BMO stadium where the LA Football Club usually sells out – It's empty. Silent. Closed.

I pass the home of the battlegrounds of the USC Trojans football team – The Coliseum is a
ghost town.
Closed.

Exposition Park is scattered with the homeless
and they are wet – angrier than usual – louder than yesterday,
and lost-
still lost.

Under the 110 expressway is a den of the dead
and I walk among them.
They can see the life in my eyes
and hear the life in my heart
as I move without fear.

I pass the Staples Center,
take a right and pass the 7th St Metro.
I head left on Hill and pass Pershing Square, the "Perch."
I Pass the Grand Central Market.
I take a right on 1st and a left on Spring.
Until I finally make it to Olvera St.

It is only me and
the zombies
alone-
unsupervised and unmasked.

The cool California air surrounds me

as I sit on my front porch and smoke *Baby Jeeter Pre-Rolled Joints* –

(Banana Kush, Grape Ape, Mojilato, Blue Zkittlez, Fire OG, Durban Poison, and Gelato 33.)

"*Premium flower, infused with*
liquid diamonds,
and dusted in kief."

What are liquid diamonds?
Who cares.

I extinguish one and
light another.

I exhale and remember LA.

I remember the golden hue that hung out
on Hollywood Boulevard at happy hour
and the smell of Dodger Dogs being cooked on the
corner of Highland while Spider-Man and Captain
Jack Sparrow fight over territory
with Marilyn Monroe and Freddy Kruger
on top of "Slash's" faded star.

I remember driving onto the back lot
of Paramount on my first job.

I remember the roar of Dodger Stadium
when we won the division
each and every year.

Go Doyers!

I remember the look of defeat of those
who crawl on hands and knees in Skid Row
and the stench of disease and depression and
dire consequences collecting their debts
from the diminished eyes that are closed
by fentanyl and foul play.

I remember walking with them daily,
a wounded lion amongst hyenas,
to remind myself of what could be.

I remember crying my eyes out on
Sunset and Vine for no reason
other than the fact that I had everything
I wanted,

it only cost me my soul.

I've been writing so much that the
words don't stop when my hands do.

From the 1st of March
I've allowed memories to dominate
reality
and in doing so have lost a grip
on it,
life.

I hear voices from the ghosts
I describe in the night after I've stopped
and I see them when I close my eyes.

I'm lost in this moment.
I'm broken in this night.
I'm falling.
I'm failing.
I'm afraid to go home.
I don't want to go home.
Where is home?

The weed makes it worse
as
the chemicals inside me slosh
into a slushy
of sloppy emotion

Make it stop.

T-minus 2 hours before departure.

Two thousand, two hundred and sixty-five miles.

Four Time Zones:
1. Pacific Standard
2. Mountain Standard
3. Central Standard
4. Eastern Standard

Eight States:
- California
- Arizona
- New Mexico
- Texas
- Oklahoma
- Arkansas
- Tennessee
- North Carolina

Google Maps says
9 days by bicycle.
35 days by foot.

33 hours by Nissan Sentra.

It is dark when I depart.

It is dark when I drive south on US-101

It is dark when I pass Silver Lake.

It is dark when I pass Echo Park.

It is dark when I use the

<table>
<tr><td>L</td><td></td><td></td></tr>
<tr><td>E</td><td></td><td></td></tr>
<tr><td>F</td><td>L</td><td></td></tr>
<tr><td>T</td><td>A</td><td></td></tr>
<tr><td></td><td>N</td><td>to merge onto the ramp to I-10 East/I-5 South</td></tr>
<tr><td>T</td><td>E</td><td></td></tr>
<tr><td>W</td><td>S</td><td></td></tr>
<tr><td>O</td><td></td><td></td></tr>
</table>

<table>
<tr><td>It is dark when I use the</td><td>R</td><td>T</td><td>L</td></tr>
<tr><td></td><td>I</td><td>H</td><td>A</td></tr>
<tr><td></td><td>G</td><td>R</td><td>N</td></tr>
<tr><td></td><td>H</td><td>E</td><td>E</td></tr>
<tr><td></td><td>T</td><td>E</td><td>S</td></tr>
</table>

to take exit 64A to
merge onto
I-15 North
toward
Barstow

Once I am on I-40 East
the sun finally rises
and if it weren't
for the millions of people
dying across the globe
this would have been an otherwise
beautiful day to be on the road.

I will stay on I-40 for the next
2,153 miles.

The desert makes the drive slow down
and the thoughts in my head
speed up - the same as my accelerator.

Blue lights appear in my rearview….
I guess the world isn't as "shut down"
as I thought.

95 in a 60

cost me
twenty
wasted minutes
and
400 dollars.

I stop for gas and it feels like I am in a
B-Level horror.

People are few.

People are silent.

Nobody Speaks.
Nobody looks you in the eye.
Nobody touches the gas pump with their bare hands.
Nobody stands close to another person.
Nobody is laughing.
Nobody is singing.
Nobody is on their phone.

Nobody.
Nobody.
Nobody.

Somebody should send this script to M. Night Shyamalan.

I take 20 more milligrams
of Adderall
purely because I have excess.

I drink one of the three Red Bulls.

My hands D
R
I
P

on the steering wheel

S
W
E
A
T

I take 20 more milligrams of Adderall

and I press on

The farther away from Los Angeles I get
the closer I get to the realization
that life as I know it is over.

The farther away I get from Hollywood
the closer I get to the realization
that I am officially unemployed.

The farther away I get from the Pacific Ocean
the closer I get to the Atlantic.

The farther away I get from that life
the closer I get to the new one.

The farther away I get from
Sunset and Vine
the closer I get to
Depot St. and Wells Grove Rd.

The farther away I get from
Santa Monica Pier
the closer I get
to "Pick'n on the Square"

The farther away I get
the more anxious I
become
as I keep getting
closer
and closer
and closer
to a world
I swore
I would
never return
to….

…closer to
Franklin North Carolina.

Delirium and paranoia
force me to stop in Oklahoma City
in the middle of the night.

Amphetamines refuse to let me sleep
but I close my eyes anyway.
I need to rest.
I need peace.
But no peace is coming.

Voices roar in my mind.
Screams.
Shouts.
Judgmental jargon on repeat.

My body pulses while
my mind rips itself away from
the car that I sit in
and howls in the night
for miles and miles
in every direction.

I am moaning on I-40

The easiest part

is that there

really is no

plan.

There is no agenda.
There is no objective.

There is only
the road and
the eye
and the relationship
between

beauty
and
death.

For as every wonder passes by,

only seen through

rearview mirrors

and dust covered

windshields,

I realize,

I am gone

I'm back

on the road

before dawn

    and I

        wish
            the
        road
would

keep going past the Appalachian

I R
mountains and C C back around.
E L

I'm not ready.
I can't.
I don't belong there.

The Tennessee Valley
mocks at me
as I resist entry.

Chattanooga gives me
a snide smirk
as I use the

L
E
F L
T A
N to take exit 185B for I-75 North
T E toward Knoxville.
W S
O

The Blue Ridge is laughing

I enter the town of Franklin at 4 PM Eastern Standard Time.

I am a shell of a human.
I am dehydrated.
I am depressed.
I am a degenerate.

I can hear my eyes screaming
with fatigue as they
pulse and throb
from staring at the interstate for
38 hours.

I am sweaty.
I am stinking.
I am sore to the touch.
I am a sack of shit.

I am welcomed by an empty house.
I am relieved by this empty house.

I'm in no state to pretend to smile.
I'm in no state to pretend to love.

My jaws hurt from grinding my teeth.
The side effects of 120 milligrams of Adderall consume me.

I am full of
amphetamines,
caffeine,
and
nicotine.

My legs shake and
my arms feel like I'm wearing concrete floaties.

My entire body pulses with every beat of my heart.
I can hear it – VWOMP VWOMMP VWOMMMP-
Vibrating.

I am vibrating.
VWOMMP VWOMMMP VWOMMMMP

like the cell phone in my pocket.

I have been awake
for
48 hours
and I am crashing.

I am full of anxiety.

I am full of doubt.

I shouldn't have come.

I need to get high.

This place is foreign to me.
This is not my childhood home.
This is not where it all came

U

N

D

O

N

E –

where it all was **R - I - P - P - E - D**

a p a r t –

the family –

or at least the idea of one.

But there is that smell from the past.
The smell of my youth walks with me as I move through this place.

The smell of my mother's cooking and smoking and drinking and absence.

That smell talks to me
as I toss and turn in my sleep.

That smell won't let me forget my past.
It has its hands around my neck

and it is choking me.

The world is closed
and I am
trapped
in rural
North Carolina.

I suppose it could be worse.
I suppose I could be
trapped
in rural
North Dakota.
or
Northern Arkansas.
Or
Northern Mississippi
or
any part of Alabama.

Yes.

It could be worse.

I spend my days
lost in nature
and my nights
lost in a haze of smoke.

The mountains
tell me that I am
unhealthy.

The mountains
shake their heads
at me in
disappointment.

Waterfalls and
blue sky revive
my eyes for a
moment but
the moments don't
last long enough.

I explore every corner of
these ancient hills.
I am
looking for answers-
looking for
myself.

But there are just
not enough.

I climb to the top of Cowee.

h
a
l   r,
u   e
t   e
I climb a   d
S   l   h,
and   a   a
S   l
u
l   o.
l   c
a   i
T   l
and   e
T

h,   r,
a   e
y   s
a   s
I climb W   e
W
and
Winding Stair Gap.

There are not enough
trails to hike and
there are not enough
mountains to climb
to fix me.

Sometimes I don't want

to

miss the sunrise or set or any other insignificant moment in between,

and

then
there

are times

that

I
want
to
close

my eyes

at

7PM
on

a

Saturday night

in
July

and

wake up

at

7AM

in
October.

My nerves keep me
from sleeping
and my heart keeps me
from dreaming
with my eyes wide open.

My fears are
on my sleeve
where my heart
usually beats and
the breath seems
to wash both
away but only
for a moment.

24 hours
in a day
leaves no time
for stretching.
24 hours
long and hard.

I want to be present
in my 24.
I want to be present-I want to be alive.
I want to breathe.

I want to begin again.

I don't think there
is such a thing as
a
"subtle
reminder."

There is only
one way of being
reminded
and it is

JARRING –

DRASTIC –

and

downright
EARTH SHATTERING.

So,

here it is.

Here is
your God Damn

reminder.

I'm not sure

exactly how

, my
younger self

would feel

about the

current version

of me - the 5.0 I'd say,

the Windows 22,
the I-Phone 34,

the Galaxy 40 Ultra.

It's not

that I am a complete

and utter

failure.

It's just

I think

he had

BIGGER PLANS

My therapist prescribes me
an animal
instead of the drugs
that tried to kill me before-
that numbed me before.

She says it will be good for me.
She says it will help.

This is the time if ever there was one.

So, I act.
I search.
And I found her.

She is 6 weeks old and all belly.
This tiny little creature.
This tiny little dog.

Her name is
Lola.

It took the friendship of a dog to
remind me how to love or
perhaps teach me to love for the
first time.

Lola taught me how to commit
and how to give without
expectation.

She taught me to have
patience.

Lola taught me that
there were better things
then drugs to keep
me company at night
and she taught me that
I wanted to be a
father.

I watch her play with admiration and jealousy.

For I too wish I could run free,

run wild,

and root around

in green grass

without a care

in the world.

In the night
she sleeps
with me,
like a child,
like a partner.

We both feel
the need
to touch
each other
for comfort.

Spooning.

The next day
my aching
shoulders
reveal my
unnatural
sleeping
positions
that cater to her
body and shape -
not my own.

Sprawling.

She is not
a morning girl
so we take our time.

Very slowly,
she'll yawn once.
Shell stretch her forelegs
and yawn again
and again.

Now she has
    risen.

She is ready
    to go.

"How you do one thing is the way you do everything"

-Martha Beck

Martha wasn't lying. I realize that I don't know
how to do anything
halfway.

I'm either all in
or I'm all out.

Speeding
or
spent.

Boiling over
or
ice cold.

I don't smoke one cigarette.
I smoke an entire pack
in one sitting.

I don't drink to feel good.
I drink to feel nothing
and I don't stop until
the lights go out.

I'm manic and I'm
obsessive.

I'm destructive.
and
I want to stop.

I'm done.
I quit.

Cold Turkey.

Am I the Ghost?
Am I the memory
that haunts?

Am I the apparition
that highlights shadows
on the eve
of
passing?

Am I the rattler
of chains
while you
sleep?

Or
the dread that
taunts?

Tell Me.

The reminders
in dreams reveal
the rectitude
of your
walk
thus far.

Mistakes

scream

louder

in your sleep

then they do

in waking life.

"I haven't forgotten you,"
they chime in,
as the visuals
of your
past
present

and
future

contort, contrive
and
continually
craft
disorienting narratives
that force
you to
wake in a

fright.

It took forty-eight nights for the cold sweats to stop.

Forty-eight nights of madness.

Forty-eight nights of nightmares
and nervousness.

Forty-eight nights of screams
in the night.

It took forty-eight nights to sleep without
towels in the bed.

Forty-eight nights without
peace.

It took forty-eight nights to purge
it all from the inside out.

Forty-eight nights that felt like an unwinnable test.

After hours

of grey

and

days

of

gloom
and
gargantuan pain

the silver lining

shimmers

through

and

light

eventually

kisses

us

back.

If you wait
long enough
the change
that you
wanted
will eventually
whisper
its
intent
to you –

It will remind
you
of the dreams
you keep
alive
and
the dreams
that
died
long ago.

Wait for it. It will come.

The voice is there
in the night
and
it remains
until early morn.

That voice is there
to remind me
to move
and not
to mull,
that voice can be
shouting
and
sharp
or
diminished
and
dull.

That voice is there
to remind me
that
there
is more.

That voice
is mine
and
it is up
to me
to heed
the advice

and toe the line.

My future is calling and I decided to respond.
Two years of Graduate School is just
on the other side of the mountain.
Two years of writing.
Two years of reading.
Two years of trying.
Two years and
hopefully
I will find a future.
Hopefully
I will find a home.
Hopefully
I will find a way –

Out.

PART II

FALLING

2022/2023

This is beyond the rabbit hole.

This
Goes

D
E
E
P
E
R

The center
of
the Earth
is just the
beginning

and
thus
is this
moment.

An origin
of
an orbital
return.

The

"X"

I *E*
N *L*
D
T *D*
H *I*
E *M*

My pen is my soul, and my story is my promised outcome.

Falling isn't failing if you
rise,
and that is what I am trying

to do –
to rise.

Again?

Or is this the first
time?

I have been here before, that place that feels foreign
feels frightful
feels foolish – almost as if this very act

is absurd.

The 40-year-old
living with mommy.
The 40-year-old
crying in bed.

The 40-year-old
waiting for the world to start over
or
perhaps the 40-year-old waiting for
it to end.

I hold it all inside and
most times it screams from within,
a seed sprouting in furious fits and fervor,
the battle that is impossible to win.

Most times it screams from within,
pain and torment echo from bone and blood,
the battle that is impossible to win,
restless nights that lend themselves to a new day's sun.

Pain and torment echo from bone and blood,
mania, heartbreak, and gut-wrenching Ire,
restless nights that lend themselves to a new day's sun,
a new day – a mouth opens wide – howling.

I've spent the last 20 years away from this place,

away from Appalachia

and these unaccelerated

A c c e n t s

and

D r a w l s

These mountains have witnessed it all.

They've seen the boy – lost in the woods,

lost in the
world,
and lost inside.
These mountains have witnessed
my childhood ripped
away
and
my heart turned cold –
my
blood filled
with fire.

These mountains have heard
me cry out for help and
heard me roar in defiance –
a rebel
repulsed.
These mountains have seen
me broken and weak
and they have seen me
at full strength – alive and
exploding with
potential.
Heartbroken and love-struck,
smitten and spiteful.

These mountains
have witnessed it all.

They've seen the boy become
the man.

Me.

Myself.

And…..
I am trying
desperately trying
not to
forget that.

In youth, Red yelled, loud – in bright shades of anger
It screamed at me and from me
Red was always pushing my world into darkness and
Taking my life – Red was relentless and rude
And rough and wrong – Red hurt – its hands around my throat.

As an adult, Red
Ran wild and was covered in sweat
From sprinting longer than everyone else
From breathing harder and faster –
Red was out of control –
A river after a rain in late
August – smelling of hurricanes and tropical storms
Wild Red – with the taste of salt on
Its tongue and the pain of salt in its wounds.

Things still move

when the wheels

fall off,

it is

just
a lot
louder

and
a
whole lot
harder.

The screech and

the
scrapes
of
metal
digging into
metal,

or
earth,

or
wood,

or anything else.

A trail of
tears
dugout
for

miles.

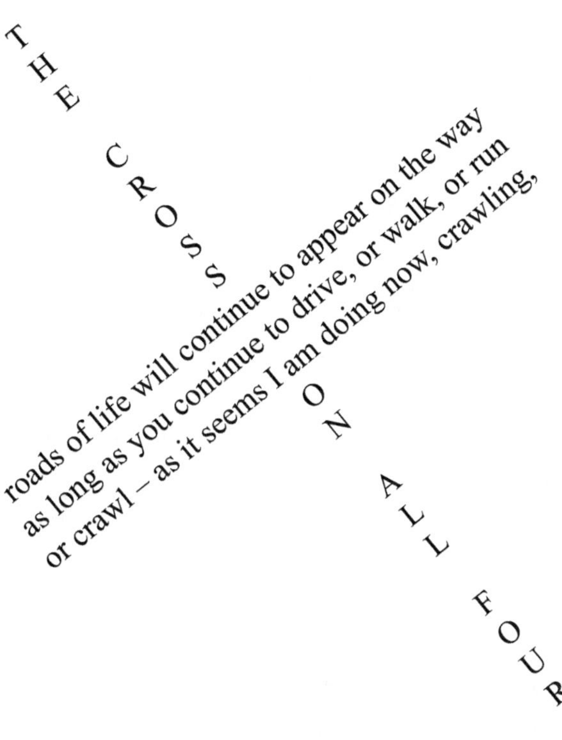
THE CROSS
roads of life will continue to appear on the way
as long as you continue to drive, or walk, or run
or crawl – as it seems I am doing now, crawling,
ON ALL FOURS

One way
A roll of the dice
Tears painted on the road
Snake eyes

Four seasons in an instant
A rotational keep

Ticking clocks count
Time well spent
Time wasted
Time stops
Time after time after time

Days are years
Years are seconds
Minutes are lifetimes

And

Lifetimes are over in the blink of an eye
Eye for an eye
Tit for Tat
Blind men see beyond the lashes of witches
and dream of grace

The sword slices deep
A paper cut
Lacerated mutations weep red
Thicker than water
Coagulated characteristics

One moment in awe
Worn out knees recite a poetic surrendering
Denim erosion
Holes are proof of life.

How many options are left? I ask myself as I smoke alone on the back porch of my mother's home.

A mother I resent.
A mother who resents me.
A mother of a brother I will never speak to again.
A mother of another brother that is not my blood.

A routine of madness.
A routine of hatred.

One after the other….

Until I pass out in a poisoned dream.
A poisoned day.
A poisoned night.
A poisoned moment.
A poisoned life.

And then I light another cigarette and gag.

Judgmental eyes of one who has no place to judge

find themselves on me

like spotlights chasing a felon on the run,

and I,
playing possum,

or dead,

because playing dead is easier
than arguing back
to the
judgmental light

that is
now
yelling in a drunken roar.

"Look at you. You're pathetic.
You're a Failure! You're nothing!
NOTHING!"

I've heard worse from better
so I pretend I'm too high
to comprehend,
too high to care,
too high to fight back - to retaliate - to tell the
truth,

to remind
the light
that it
is not natural,
the only way that this light exists
is to be plugged in,
turned on –

You know what they say…an opioid a day

keeps the doctors…
re-prescribing. And you think it's light.

FAILURE: / feyl-yer / noun

1. an act or instance of failing or proving unsuccessful; lack of success:
   His effort ended in failure

2. nonperformance of something due, required, or expected:
   a failure to do what one has promised; a failure to appear

3. a subnormal quantity or quality; an insufficiency:
   a failure of crops

I suppose I could place myself
in one of the three
examples listed
above.

It just sounds worse when
she says it,
her,
mom,
the woman who hasn't come close
to achieving what I have.

But then I ask myself,
what have I achieved?

In the past seven years, I have succeeded
in staying alive.

I also failed at
taking my own life
on more than one occasion.

Does that make me successful
at staying alive?
Or a failure at taking it?

What have I achieved?
And does achievement
determine success?

I would almost always have answered yes,
until now as I find myself waiting
for my mother to serve me dinner and judge me after.

I have been here too long.

My forty-year-old
tears trickle down
and Lola,

she can feel my pain
and she moves
closer to me
with aid.

She comes closer to me
with softened eyes
and a softer mane.

I see her and wonder
how I can love
an animal more
than a mother
her child.

And she comes closer.

She can feel my pain.

And she responds-

With love.

I escape with exercise.

I rise before dawn to move until the night.

Only to undo all the work at night
by smoking Camel Blues
and
homegrown
Lemon Kush
until I
pass
out.

I'm manic you see.
I cannot do something
unless I do it to the

EXTREME.

I don't exercise three times a week
I do it seven days a week,
twelve hours
a day.

I don't swim laps,
I swim miles.

I don't run miles,
I run for days.

There comes a time when I
cannot do anything
more
than move my body
because

the idea of being
stationary

makes
me
want
to

P
uk
e

The classroom is my way out or a way up or a way around this stalled moment in time.

The college hidden in the smoky safety of a rural Carolina landscape,
over the mountain, "Cowee Mountain" to be exact, and through the woods, the "Blue Ridge"
to be exact –

To graduate school I go, "WCU" to be exact.

Is this Plan B?

Is this even a plan?

It feels more like the only
way to justify
my
presence here

and my only way to justify
the return
and the redundancy
and the reinvention of myself.

No –
Scratch that.
This is not a
reinvention,

This is a
REBRANDING
A change in font.

This is a
reason.

And this will hopefully work.

Or else…

Ah, this feels
oddly familiar -

This feeling
of
excitement
mixed with

caution –

The moment before
you
step
off
the
ledge,

or perhaps

better
said,

A
E p

L
from
the
cliff.

All that is left now is
to
free

F

A

L

L

I read every assigned page
until I find myself
in the library
with my head
slung back

with my

T H W
U I
O D
M E

O N

P E

while I snore
the rhetoric
of
Aristotle,
Loyd Bitzer,
Mignolo,
Lauren Cagle,
Vatz,
Scott Consigny
and
Edbauer.

Theory
to shake the cobwebs.

Nine P.M.

The class is released
and something catches
my eye.

The light.
I always notice
the light.

And the light tonight is
painting auras of
white,
orange,
and
blue
on the mountainside.

The painted light
guides me
home,
but it is not my
own
and I miss the
life I
once
had.

I miss it.
I miss the city light. I miss Los Angeles.

The glow of neon
and spotlight
and bars overflowing with
booze
on
Hollywood
Boulevard with the smell of barf
suffocating my nose.

I miss Chicago.
I miss the Ukrainian
Village,
the place
I used
to call
home.

N
U T
O A
M I
the N.

over
drive
I
So,

To somebody else's home.
NOT my own.
And I do it in
silence
as I remember
the
light.

To shape glass

or

metal
the
temperature has to be

1200 degrees fahrenheit –

beyond so
even.

It's got
to
be

molten.
The same goes

for

man.

In order to

be
shaped into something
of
value
one must
be
thrown into fire.

Only after will we
see

what he, or
I,

or you or them – or we

was or is
meant to become.

A break comes and gives me time
to reflect on
the death of a friend.

A perfect life taken
in a flash.

This one hurts more
for some reason.

This one won't leave my
mind, won't leave my body.

I hadn’t smoked since the
school year
began –

I was trying to
keep a
clear head.

But a break gave me time
to reflect on
a death of a friend
and I didn’t like what I saw.

Grief looks different
on
different
people.

On me….
It looked
like
seven days of smoking
non-stop.
From sunrise to the end of the night,
whenever that
was.

I was trying
to solve the
mystery of
death in
every inhale of weed and
tobacco.

Yet, all the while
finding myself
even more lost
even more confused
even more heartbroken
even more nauseous
even more angry

And even more stoned.

We don't see ourselves
bleed
enough.
That is our problem.

We forget the feeling
of being cut wide open.

We forget the color
of
the one thing that
fills us - The deep dark

R

I

V within us.

E

R

We need more blood.
We need more reminders of
mortality
to help us run from
the

Mundane
Muted
Monotone
Miserable
Monotonous
Melancholy
Melodramatic
Mutinous

life
we
claim to be living.
I want to bleed.

I come to you as a soldier at war.
Somehow alone, somehow alive, somehow in love.
In this place, I am erased and on bent knee, I pray for peace.
Can such a future exist for the wretched? Or a heart full of hate?
Or do our destinies live out on pages and lines without change,
Without promise or possibility of growth, is it impossible to evolve?

What does it mean to truly evolve?
Does that mean an ending to the blood-filled war?
Does that mean that we are fated to change?
Or does it mean that broken hearts of hate will always return to love?
Screams that echo madness mirror truths of unrelenting hate.
But in the end, the truth is told and through tears, we live in peace.

In this place, reality is lost and yet we speak of peace
Creating a cliché that creeps in and prevents the prose the ability to evolve.
This is why we stumble here and fall in fits of hate
Because this is not a place of kindness at all, but a location of war.
Empty lines birth fulfilled lusts – a union made in love
And in the end, its the truth that lies and words refuse to change.

Words don't just appear in this place, this place that begs for change,
No, they have been flying for years now birthed in fevers of peace.
That is when the possibility of reunion ignites, combined with hopes of love
That is when we read out loud the story of how we can evolve.
Fields of blood and bone are here and remind us of the war,
And in doing so return our heart to page one – the moment before the change.

This is not meant to be pretty and I'm sure it's really meant for hate,
This world we live in – here and now – is impossible to change.
Lines weren't meant for peace and harmony but instead a violent war
A place of vileness and lost virtue perhaps, and a place in need of peace,
But peace does not come free for us nor does it promise to evolve,
yet we enter still with shaky legs and hearts that remember to love.

Come here you impossible thing – come closer to those who love,
Come close to the fire of the prose no matter how much you think you hate,
And listen to the story that is told to you – a story that promises to evolve
Words on the page don't come without pain and they always lend themselves to change
Even though this battle will never end and you will never find peace
The act itself is beautifully refined and nothing but a prophesied war.

I don’t rest my hat
on my ability to beguile.
I don’t trust my mouth
to follow suit.

But I do trust
my legs to do the
lifting my arms cannot,
allowing me to get
closer to the truth.

There may not be calluses
on the palms of my hands,
nor many blisters bubbled up
from wear and tear,

But my soul has been
hardened by more than
mere labor, exceeding that of
which
bear.
the average man can

The bottom is cold.
The light – white and cold.
The closer I stay at the bottom
the closer I can be to the light,
the only light there is.

White and cold and blue and
reflecting off of a wet surface.
Above me, a lifetime of darkness,
compressing me and pushing me.
So, I press deeper into the bottom,
the only light there is –

I dig my fingers into it
And try to pull myself down inside
to become the bottom itself.
The bottom is pock-marked.
Drastically aged.
Ancient bricks, two inches by six,
that line the life that I am in,
and reflecting the light,
the only light there is.

Finding your footing

doesn’t always
determine

whether
you

F
A
L
L

or not.

Sometimes, just when you feel

like you’re planted

firmly,

you blink, and

before you know it,

you

are

T
U
M
B
L
I
N
G

face first back down from
where you came.

You know as well as I do,

the speed of it all.

The swirl of a moment becomes a
rotation of time;
of days, months, years.

Blink – it's new

Blink – it's old

Blink – it's forgotten

Blink – it's remembered

Time will play tricks on those
unaware,
as it seems to slow to snails pace
in times of woe
or
seems to stop
in the arms of love.
But don't be fooled
for one moment – you see time
is not on our side

and it is
speeding
up – faster and faster
the more we
blink.

All the days and all the nights,
all the smiles and all the
fights –

It happened so fast.

A successful first year of school
brings me to my knees, on fumes – burnt out. e like
I stand knee-deep in k a
o diesel engine
ash m low on
while I continue to s oil.

I look around and wonder
if this was the right
move.

Was this the right choice? Will I succeed?
Will I fail?

Memories of what
was impede upon
what can be

and I cannot help but
think
of the life
I once had.

Or better said,

the life
I was trying
to have.

I look around as if I was a lotus eater
just roused from a seven-year sleep and ask, how did I get here?

A new day creates new mornings
as a 4 AM wake-up becomes the new norm.

There is time in the dark hours of the morning
that give me time to listen
and give me time to pray.

My knees found their place on solid ground
as my heart begs for forgiveness
and beg for
peace.

And with

A Y
R K
M S
S

E
R H
A T
I
S
E O
D T

I
Surrender

Dear Lord,
I come to you to ask for forgiveness.
Lord, I pray that you will fill me with your light and love
and surround me with grace.
Lord, I am grateful for all that you have given me
and I give thanks to you.
This is enough, my Lord.
You are enough.
Lord God, you have blessed me.

Jesus, I pray that you will continue to stay with me,
To guide me and speak to me when I am lost.
Jesus, please fill my heart and let me
be a reflection of you to the world that surrounds me.

Lord God, I pray that will keep me safe
from ailment and injury and be a force against evil
as it forms itself around me.
Lord God, bless those that I love and protect them
but even more so God,
bless my enemies.
Lord, bless my enemies more than you bless me.
God find them and fill their hearts
so that they may know
the love of God
and turn from their ways.

In Jesus' name.

Amen

PART III

FAITH

2023/2024

The water
has been calling me,
for a lifetime perhaps,
or maybe just since my soul went
dry.

The water finds me
in the night
as I attempt to sleep
in sweat-covered nightscapes
that remind me of all that I have lived, lost, and longed for.

The water has always given me peace
and now it promises even more, eternal life,
as I am in desperate need of regeneration and renewal

As I wade into a mountain-fed pool of living spirit, bubbling, raging, flowing.
I know that the water is inside of me as the energy charges
from my toes upward through my legs, to my core,
through my lungs, up through my chest
like an electrical current set in motion
rioting through my neck
and throat until it finds my mouth and
escapes in an exhalation
of awe and prayer.

I give myself to the water.
I am submerged in the love of God.
I am forgiven.

I am free.

Water baptized and born again.

The warmth
of summer

lends itself
to adventurous
invitations

with someone
new.

As Needmore
releases us,

her and I,
H

into the *T*

R

Tennessee river *O*

N

as her and I float

toward
Lake Fontana.

We navigate
the river

as we navigate
ourselves,

trying to understand if
our feelings are valid –

They are.

Just as you are strong
enough
to control the tides,
you
have thus controlled us.

Sent us to you.
For you.
With you.

A union of the flesh
and
full moon –

full enough.

Full enough to fill a sky with possibility.

Full enough to
fill a sky with
predestined
prose.

Full enough to see her skin shine
like illuminated
reflections
of
water,
stars,
of you.

We give ourselves
to the moment
and
allow you to guide our
every move
until
you disappear and return
full again,

super
and
new.

Have you ever

P
looked U

to the sky
in the midst
of a mizzle?

Looked into the eyes
of clouds
as they
rain down into yours?

Felt the D and D
R R
I O
P P
S S

of water
enter your soul
in the middle of
July?

Or

tasted the mist of
icy mountain water
mixed
with
sun showers
warmed by the
midday sun?

Close your eyes
and imagine
how beautiful it was.

It took the very
best of
you -“I”
to make me,

or perhaps
the
very
worst.

The strength.
The charm.
The smiles.
The harm.

The addictive nature.

The selfishness and sloth.

The
life
and
the death
of
you - “I”
made
every bit of me.

Two Sides/Two Lives.

Too many times.

I ran away from you
And swore I'd never come back
But you knew all along that I'd return
To the worn-out trail that was created by him
That leads me to something money can't buy
Lying down, looking upward, at everything new

Old seasons return and bring something that I once knew
Like a photograph or a reflection of life, a mirror image of you
Left over memories and mayhem that forgot to say goodbye
Mile after mile, you lead me forward and back
You've given something special, and we owe it all to him
Year after year, destined to return

Forty years in the future, only one thing is left to return
A lifetime ago, I promised I would bring you someone new
Even though the plan has been written by him
The path unwalked still begs me to stray, and I know that is coming from you
I've crossed the ridges while leading, and I've followed from the back
And every time I've noticed you watching, idly standing by

Another incline tells me that time's running out and that it's something I wish I could buy
But I know that borrowed minutes of a wasted life is nothing I could return
No store credit, no exchanges, not one cent of your money back
The only thing worth doing is the thing that's completely new
And that goes for the mountain, especially when the mountain is you
Together we climb, and together we fall on our knees to him

I will now try to rise, and climb upward for you and for him
Even though I know that I'm destined to say goodbye
I feel better knowing I spent my last days with you
In the next life, perhaps I'll be there waiting for your return
And the trailhead will whisper something completely new
Just promise that you won't quit halfway and that you will remember the way back

You've been there my entire life, and I have learned to use the switchback
Side to side, I'll gradually climb, and eventually come closer to him
A day in the life of a hiker looking for nature to give something new
Morning sunlight that catches your eye and begs nothing of any passerby
As sunset falls, I am doomed to trust in its return
The same way I waited for the boy to become you

If indeed our time is finite,
ticking by
second by
second,
minute by minute,
day by day –

Why is it that we
pause?
Why is it that we
are so afraid to jump?
Headfirst from the highest
vantage point
should be our life's purpose.

Yet we can find ourselves
crawling low, ankle deep
wading through our
existence until
all fades to black.

Shake yourself free of
the fear of falling
and eliminate your excuse
to *NOT* entertain every single
experience that
is meant for
you.

Seek.
All things
need to be
sought out for life
to give us what we
need in order to grow,
in order for us to look back on
days lived with at least one tear of
joy that reminds us that we felt it.
Life – abundantly and minutely
Life – a feeling of hope and trust
Life – a feeling of loss and love and love lost
Tears reflect truth in rearview mirrors without lying
yet objects appear closer than they seem while driving fast.

By merely writing
it makes it relevant.
A date written in time.
A happening acknowledged as such.
A moment of recollection and insight,
of ignorance and pride.

Self-reflection thrust upon
the only mirror that shows truth.
A lifelong dialogue
suppressed to episodes in time
gushing and devouring every second
only to be pulled back
once again,
like tides,
the never-ending
ebb and flow.

I dream of the endless flow.
The sacrifice,
the scars,
the sentiments sleighed on lines,
on pages –

in hearts.

A summer filled
sun soaked and
splashing in nature and time
makes it hard to
return to academia,
hard to return
to curriculums
and class work.

Yet still, there is a want;
a need to continue,
a drive to finish
and a curiosity to
see what will happen next.

Will I lead well?
Will I be a good teacher?
Mentor?
Leader?

Will I create work that
I'm proud of?
Will I create work worthy
of publishing or printing?
Or even sharing?

Summer is over.

It's time to go back.

It's time to finish what I started.

To pursue is to acknowledge a want,
and act in a manner in which to achieve it –
no matter the outcome.
or perhaps because of the outcome.

The best part of the story ….
the anticipation.
When the idea of what's being
said or written
excites just as much
as the moment
of its existence.

It is not the result of the pursuit
that matters but more specifically,
the tenacity in which I pursue,
that informs the world
of my intentions
and more importantly –
my guile.

These are the nights
that will make a difference
merely because it is being done
an awareness that allows
me to say to myself –

"I am a writer.
I am someone who
is graced with an ability –
no – an affinity –
to comprehend the
relentless rambles of
consciousness and attempt –
no - aggregate –
the completion of thought."

An acknowledgment to self
that pronounces proximity to the divine.
Men who dream of godliness
die enslaved to its pursuit. And so, like Icarus toward the Sun…

I fly

There is something

inside of me

that prefers

to be a tyro

in lieu of

being trained,

I'd rather

be green,
a novice.

For how exciting

it all is –

to learn

to grow

to evolve

and to be a student

in pursuit

of knowledge.

I prefer to surround myself with the passionate.
Those who crave and those who cry;
those who go a little crazy before they die.

I want energy and excitement that cannot be dulled.
I want enthusiasm that ignites fires and fuels furnaces;
burning light that never grows cold.

I love the look of the focused,
eyes that pull upward for more.

I love the sound of the hungry
and heartfelt echoing lions roar.

I can sense my own kind,
recognize familiar traits in the DNA.

I am a wild animal going after what I want.
I was born this way.

Poetry

and

short stories,

novels
and
the
truth,

fill a semester with

inspiration

as

Suarez,
Suess,
Singleton,
and
Smart,

Palahniuk
and
Petrisino,

McClarney
and
McConaughey;

Donaldson,

Hopler,

Mailer,

Rash,

and

more

show me the way.

As I stand before 22 students
that are 22 years younger,
I see emptiness
in their eyes and
hear reluctance in their mouths.

Silence.

Staring.

Am I intimidating them?
Or are they intimidating me?

My companion Lola, the service animal at my feet,
helps break the ice.

A student asks, "Why do you need a service animal?"

I tell the truth with the hope that
my vulnerability will gain their trust.

"For PTSD support," I respond.

They accept my answer.

They accept me.

It takes weeks
to get them to talk
as silence fills
room 203 on
Mondays - Wednesdays and Fridays
from 12:20 to 1:10.

I want them to love
this as much as I do
and then I have to remind myself
that they have their own paths,
and their own wants –
their own passion.

22 students and not
one English major.

Still, I urge them to create.

With pen in hand, they write daily and I beg them not to stop.

The change of seasons brings back
familiar feelings;

feelings that
don’t
make sense.

Feelings meant for
something
worse.

But still,
the fall and winter
bring depressing
tendencies
and
sadness.

I fight the urge
to return
to
manic ways
as a voice
of weakness
calls
out to me
from within;

a voice
that has
controlled me
in the past,

a voice that has
led me
astray,

a voice of
evil
plotting
my demise.

A goal
keeps
my eyes
looking
forward

as my
PhD
application
has been
submitted.

There is
nothing
to do
now
but wait
and
pray.

The winter solstice awakens
my bones and my breath
as I find my way back to
the water,
back to movement
back to the beginning.

One step at a time,
one stroke,
one lap,
one mile,
one day.

My answers to misery
have always been found
in motion as
sweat reminds me
what I am
made of
and
made for
while
my mind
contemplates
and
questions,
considers
and
craves.

The Florida sun
performs CPR
to my soul
and I am
reawakened,
refocused,
reanimated,
reminded
and
ready
for
whatever
may come.

I cry for my future

and the possibility of what I will become

and I cry for my past.

I cry for the man who was broken.

I cry for the man that I am.

I cry out of happiness.

I cry out of love.

I
cry
and
I
cry
and
I
cry
and
I
cry
and
I
cry
and
I
cry
and
I
cry

Tears were only meant

for moments like this;

for dreams that come true,

for prayers answered.

I stand on
unfamiliar ground.

Ground that is
stable, firm, -
a solid foundation.

All of my life
it has felt like
the ground
would give way
at any moment

Like it would *c-r-u-m-b-l-e* beneath my feet.

Until now.

It took
falling
and
failing
time and time again
to get to this moment,
this place in time,
this opportunity.

It took breakdowns, blunders, and b
a
c
k
s
l depression
i and
d defeat.
e
s,

Ultimately,
it took hitting the bottom,
flat on my face
to find my purpose,
find progress,
find my faith,
and find peace.

ACKNOWLEDGMENTS

I would like to thank Dr. Catherine Carter for her level of creative commitment, compassion, and support. I would also like to thank my mother and her husband, Mary and Mike Spaid, for giving me a room in their home and a place to escape to during the COVID-19 pandemic. I must also acknowledge Chris and Kenny Davis for their love and unwavering support, and Virgil Suarez for "driving the bus."

ABOUT THE AUTHOR

Braulio Fonseca is a writer, educator, veteran, and endurance athlete whose work explores resilience, vulnerability, and the transformative power of starting again. Raised in the mountains of Appalachia. His writing is deeply shaped by a sense of place—by the rugged landscapes, tight-knit communities, and quiet perseverance that define the region. That early understanding of endurance, humility, and belonging continues to inform his literary voice.

A PhD candidate in Creative Writing at Florida State University and Managing Editor of *The Southeast Review*, Fonseca writes at the intersection of lyrical inquiry and lived experience. His work blends intimate reflection with intellectual depth, examining how identity fractures and reforms after moments of profound upheaval.

Before fully turning to the literary life, Fonseca served in the U.S. military—an experience that sharpened his understanding of discipline, brotherhood, mortality, and purpose. Later, as a two-time cancer survivor, he was forced into another kind of reckoning, learning firsthand how quickly the body can become both battlefield and teacher. These defining chapters of his life animate *Falling Forward*, a memoir concerned less with the fall itself than with the courage required to rise with greater awareness.

Fonseca is the founder of Smoky Mountain Storytellers, a live storytelling series dedicated to cultivating literary community and expanding access to the arts in Western North Carolina. Whether on the page, in the classroom, or in the water as an open-water swimmer, he is guided by the belief that falling is not failure but forward motion.

In *Falling Forward*, Fonseca invites readers to reconsider the narratives we inherit about hardship and recovery, suggesting that the most meaningful lives are not those untouched by fracture, but those willing to be remade by it.

www.ingramcontent.com/pod-product-compliance
Lightning Source LLC
LaVergne TN
LVHW081301100826
845148LV00005B/938
9798899330216